RIGHTSTART™ MATHEMATICS

by Joan A. Cotter, Ph.D.

LEVEL A
WORKSHEETS

Printed in the United States of America

www.RightStartMath.com

For more information:
info@RightStartMath.com

Supplies may be ordered from:
www.RightStartMath.com
order@RightStartMath.com

Activities for Learning, Inc.
321 Hill St.
Hazelton, ND 58544-0468
888-272-3291 or
701-782-2000
fax 701-782-2007

ISBN 978-1-931980-25-8

January 2012

Game Log

Math Games are an important part of the RightStart™ Mathematics program. Instead of math drills or flashcards, we encourage you to play Math Card Games with the child. The manuals include many games and suggest additional games in the Review and Practice lessons (Levels C to E). For additional games, refer to the *Math Card Games* book.

This game log will help you keep a record of the games you play and when you played them. To help memorization, repetition is essential. Games must be played frequently. Games will help the child practice and apply math skills, especially the facts.

Date	Game Played	Players

Game Log

Date	Game Played	Players

Games help children understand, apply, and enjoy mathematics.

Name _______________________________

How many?

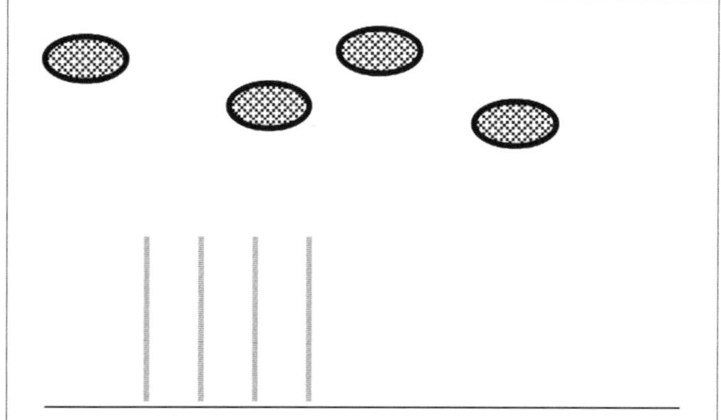

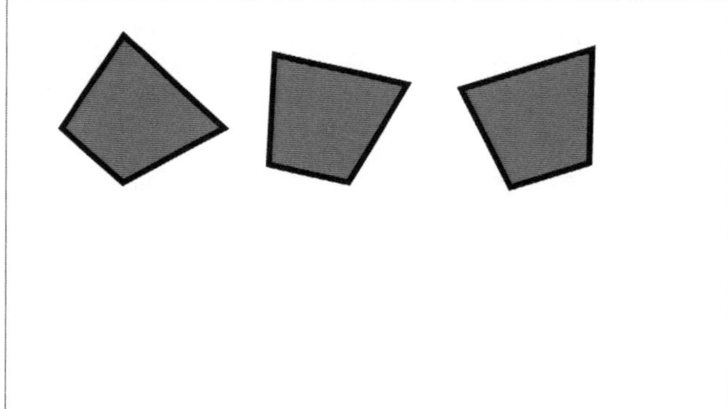

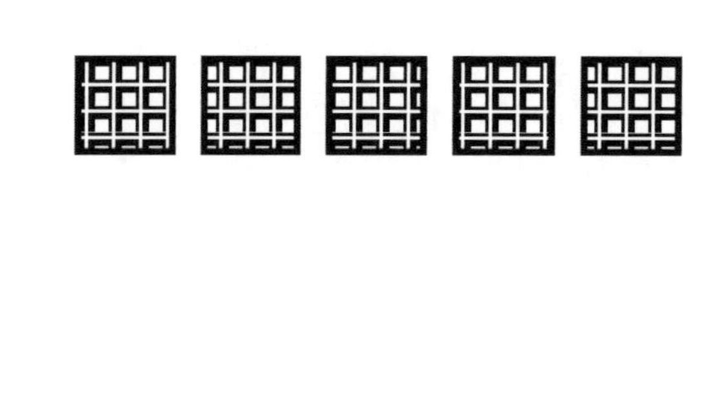

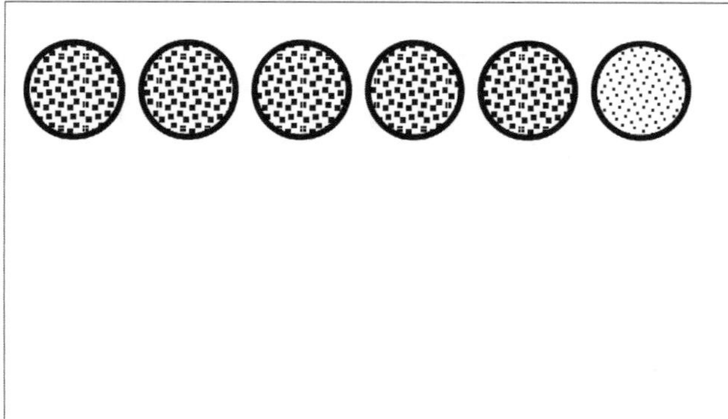

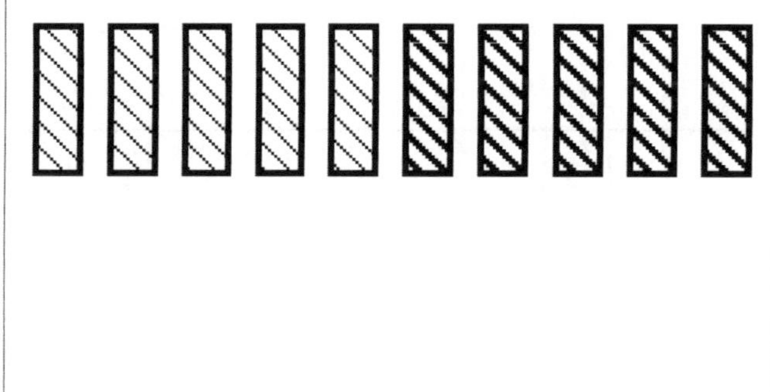

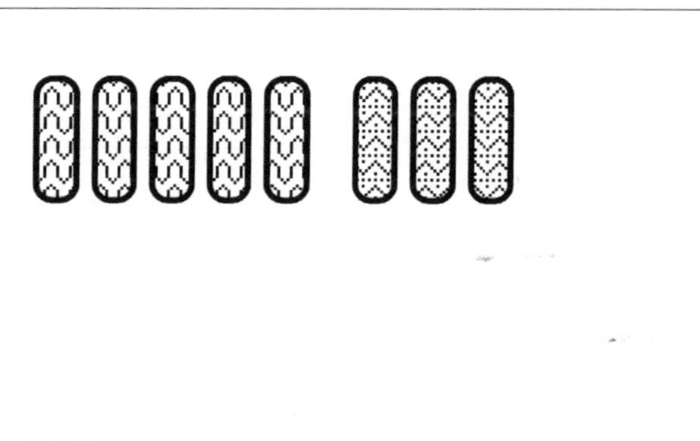

Name ____

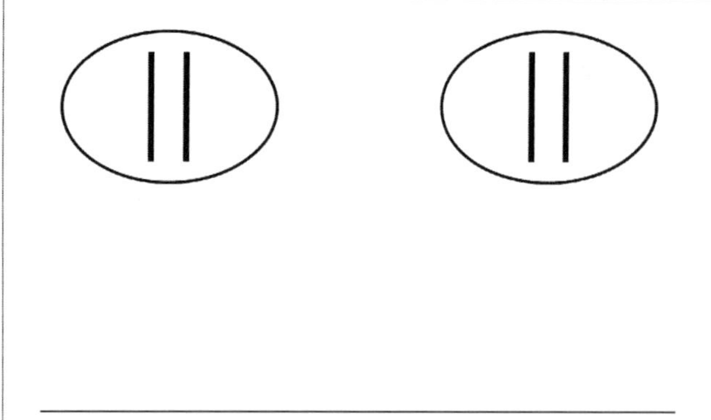 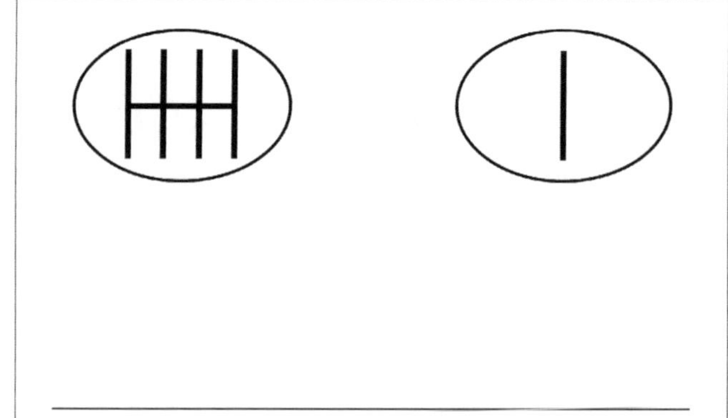

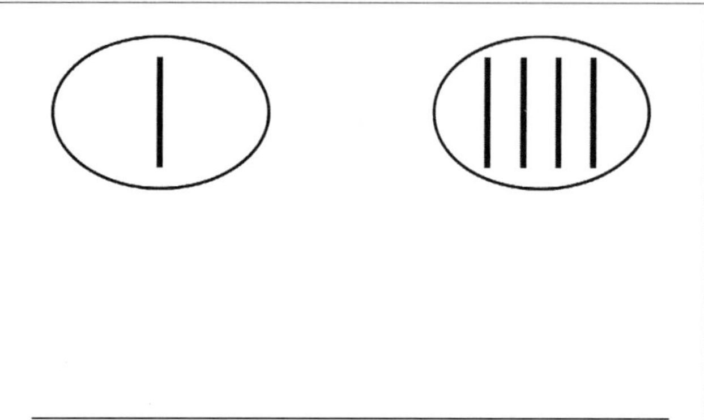 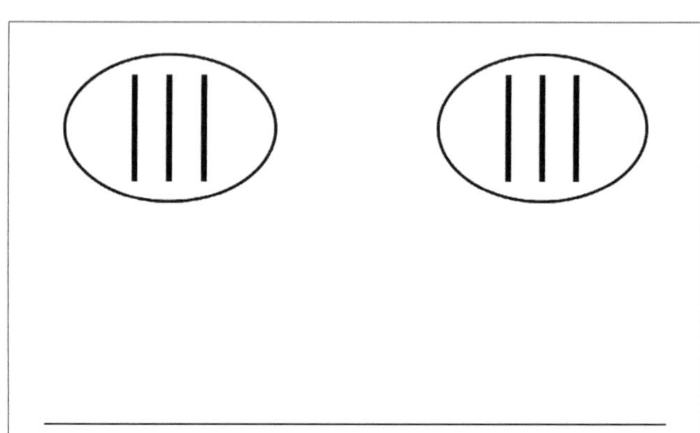

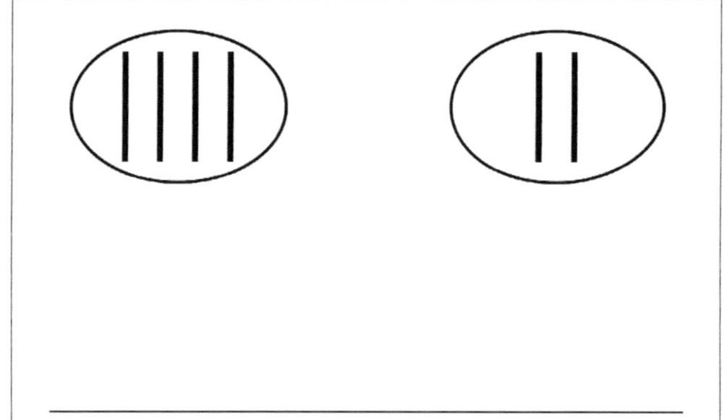 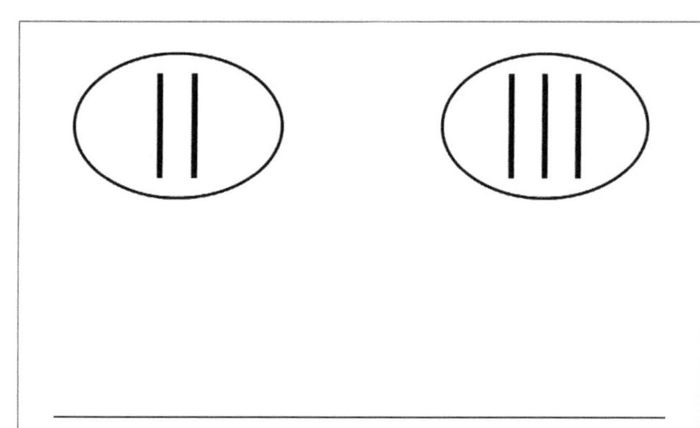

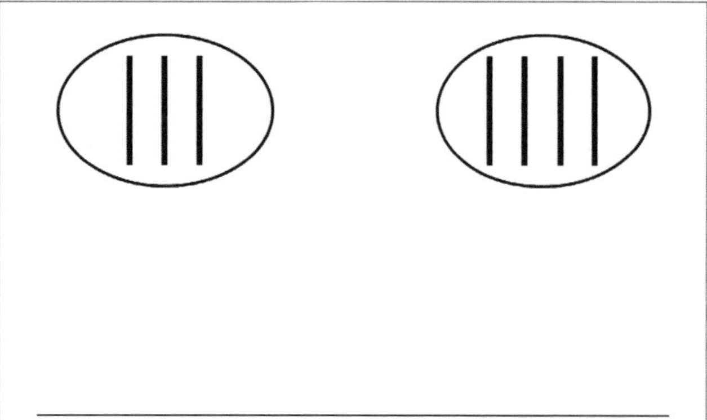 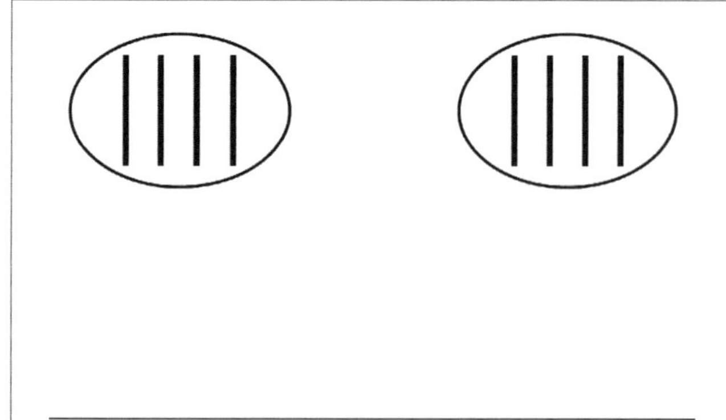

Name ____

Name ____

Name ___________

Name ___________

Name ____

Circle or color the tens.

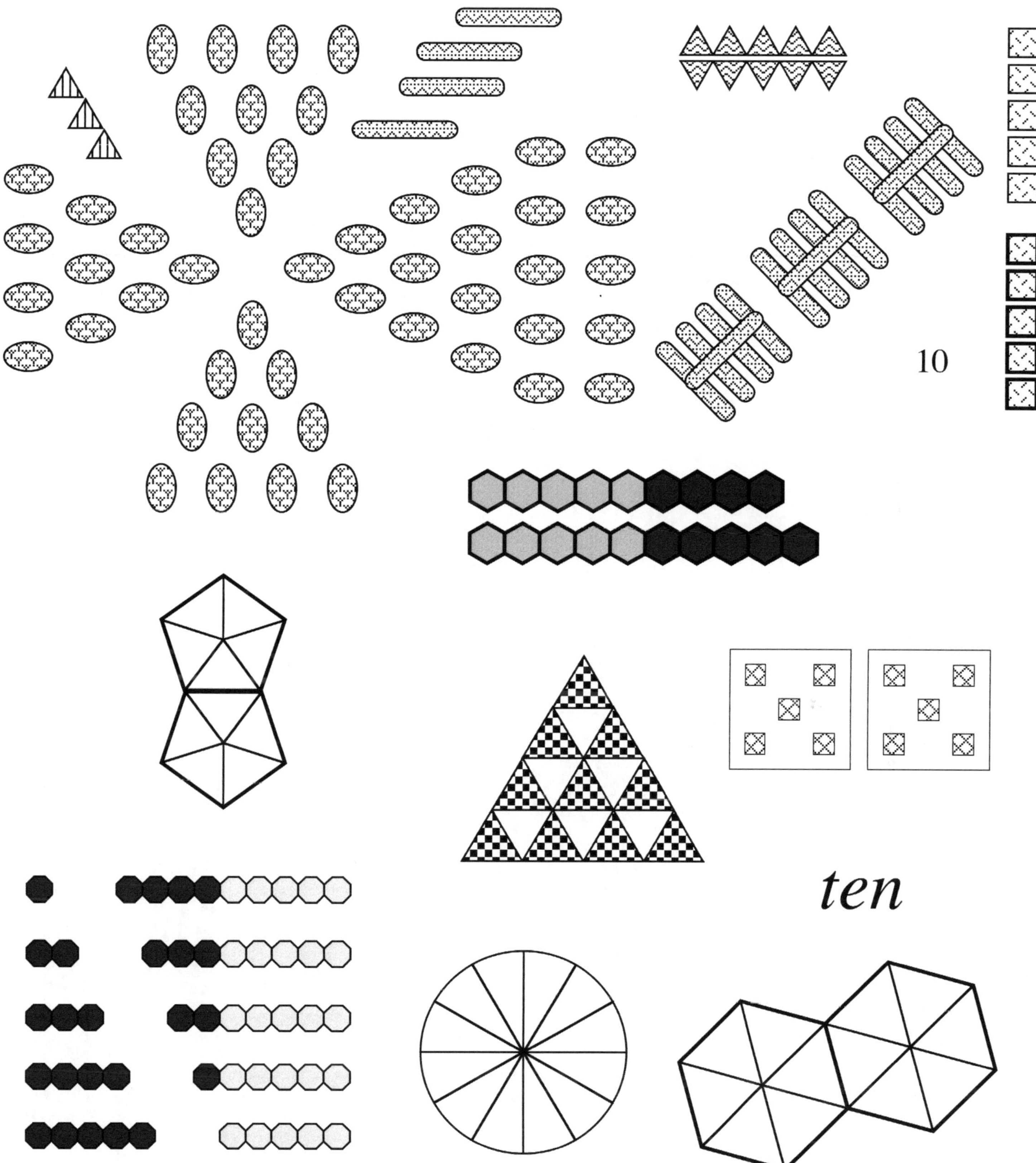

Name ______________________________

Name ______________________________

Name ______

Name ______

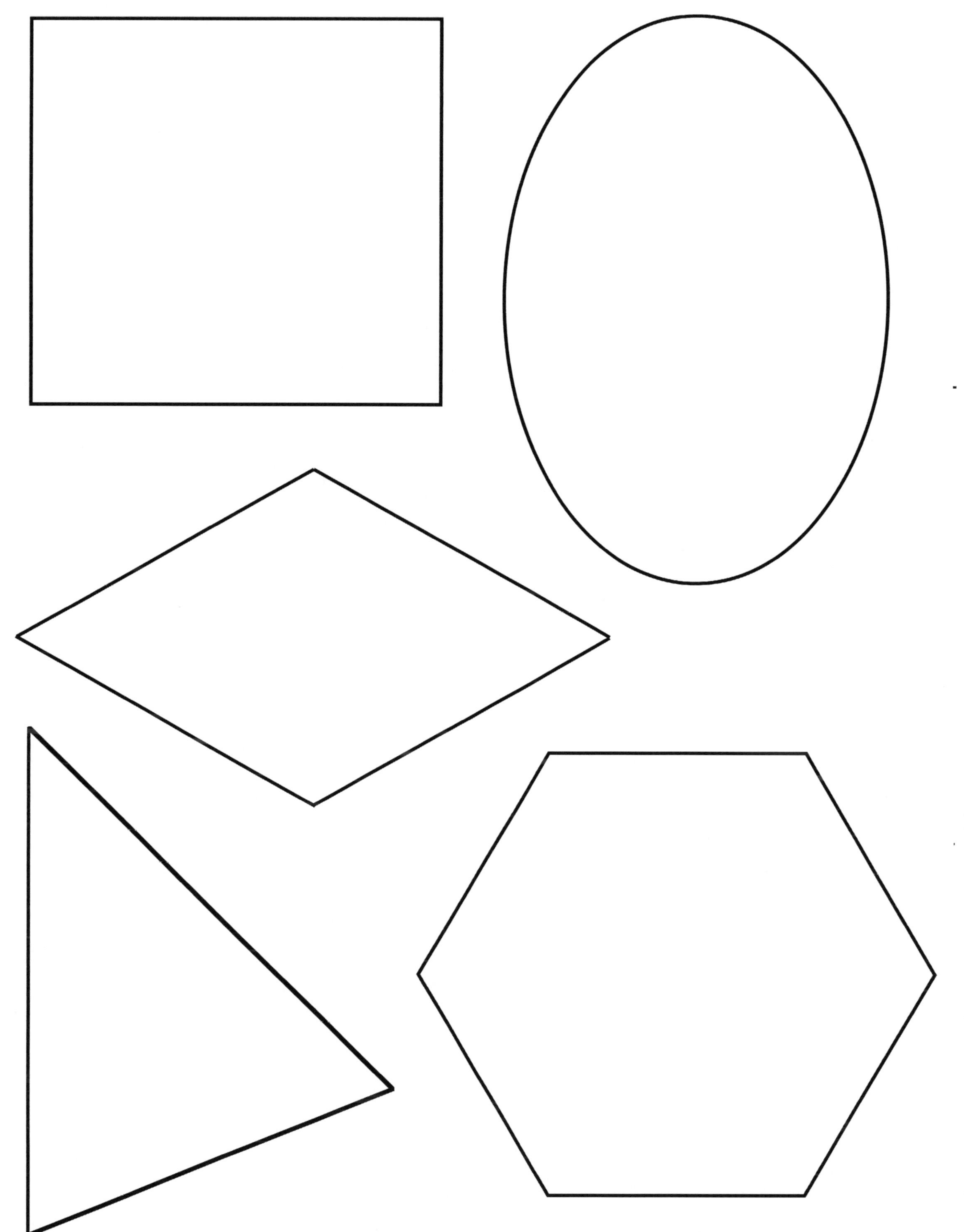

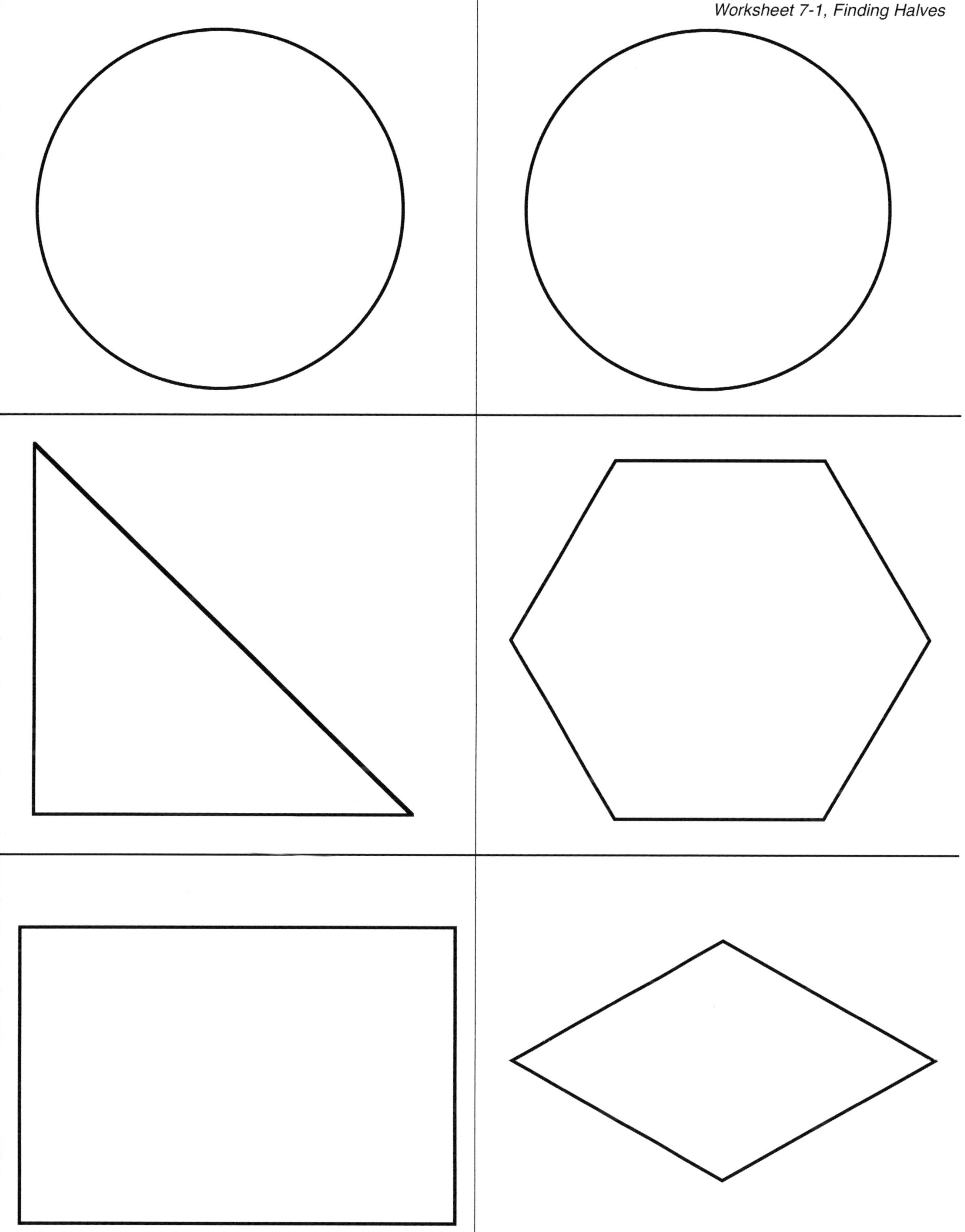

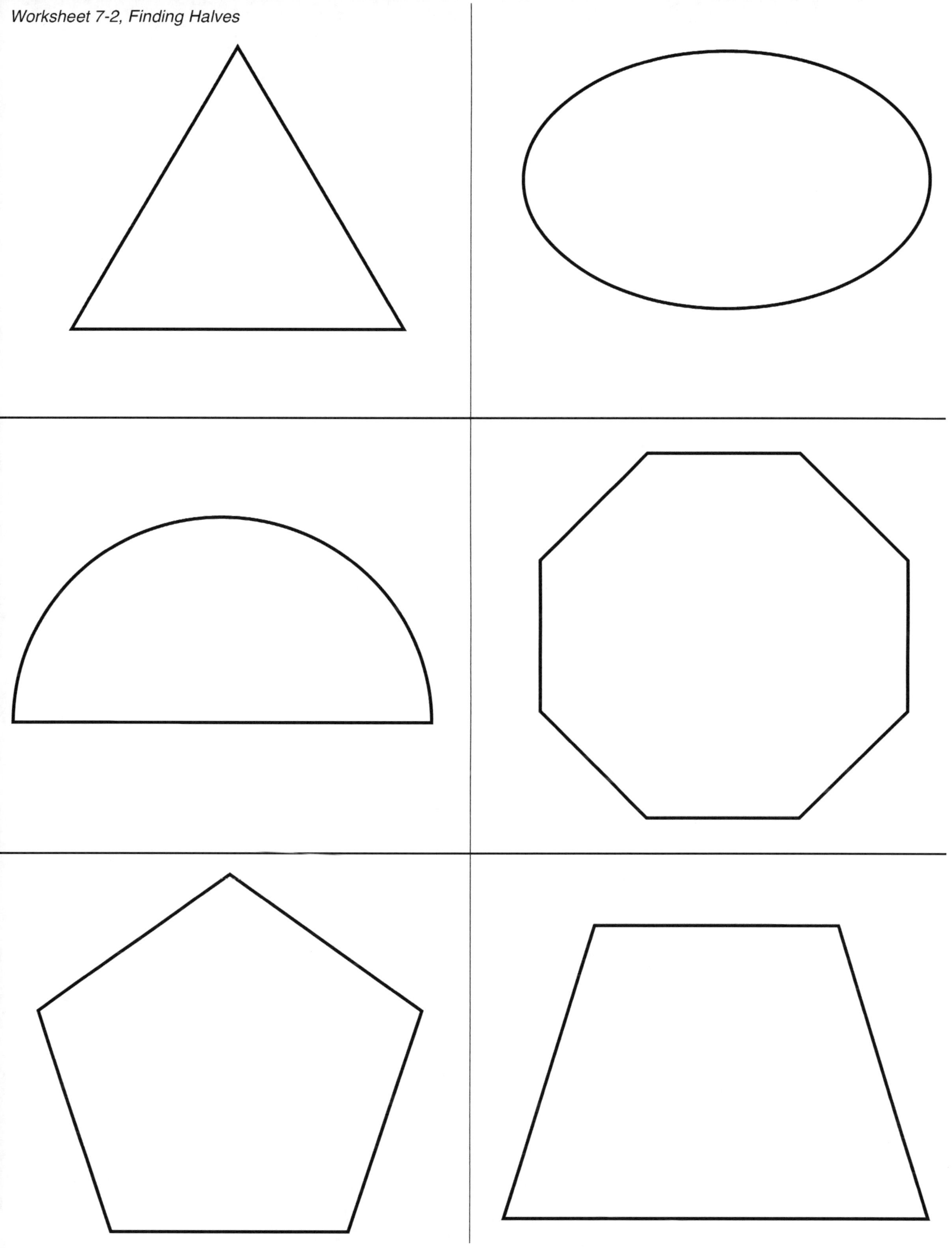

Name ___________

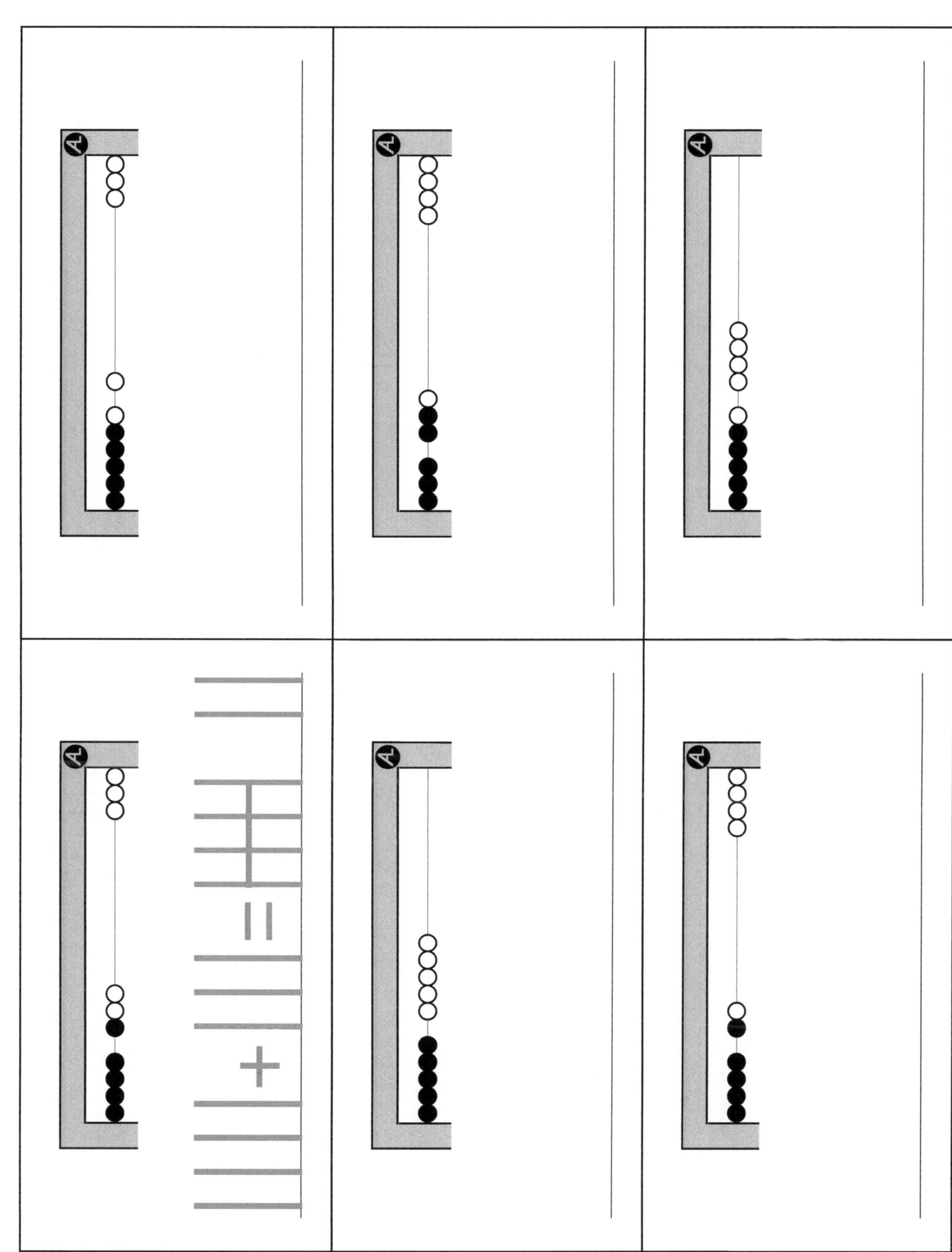

6 + 1 =

Name

Worksheet 10-1, Adding with the Abacus

Name ________

1 + 3 =
3 + 7 =
3 + 5 =
2 + 4 =
1 + 6 =
4 + 5 =
1 + 2 =
0 + 5 =

Name ________

2 + 1 =
4 + 1 =
1 + 1 =
5 + 1 =
9 + 1 =
7 + 1 =
3 + 1 =
6 + 1 =

Worksheet 13, Ten Equals

Name ___________

10 = 9 + ___
10 = 7 + ___
10 = 4 + ___
10 = 8 + ___
10 = 2 + ___
10 = 6 + ___
10 = 5 + ___
10 = 3 + ___

Worksheet 12-2 Adding Ones

Name ___________

5 + 1 = ___
4 + 1 = ___
6 + 1 = ___
8 + 1 = ___
7 + 1 = ___
2 + 1 = ___
9 + 1 = ___
3 + 1 = ___

Name ______________________________

Cut apart the tens and ones and the numbers on the heavy lines.
On other paper, glue four numbers and the matching tens and ones.

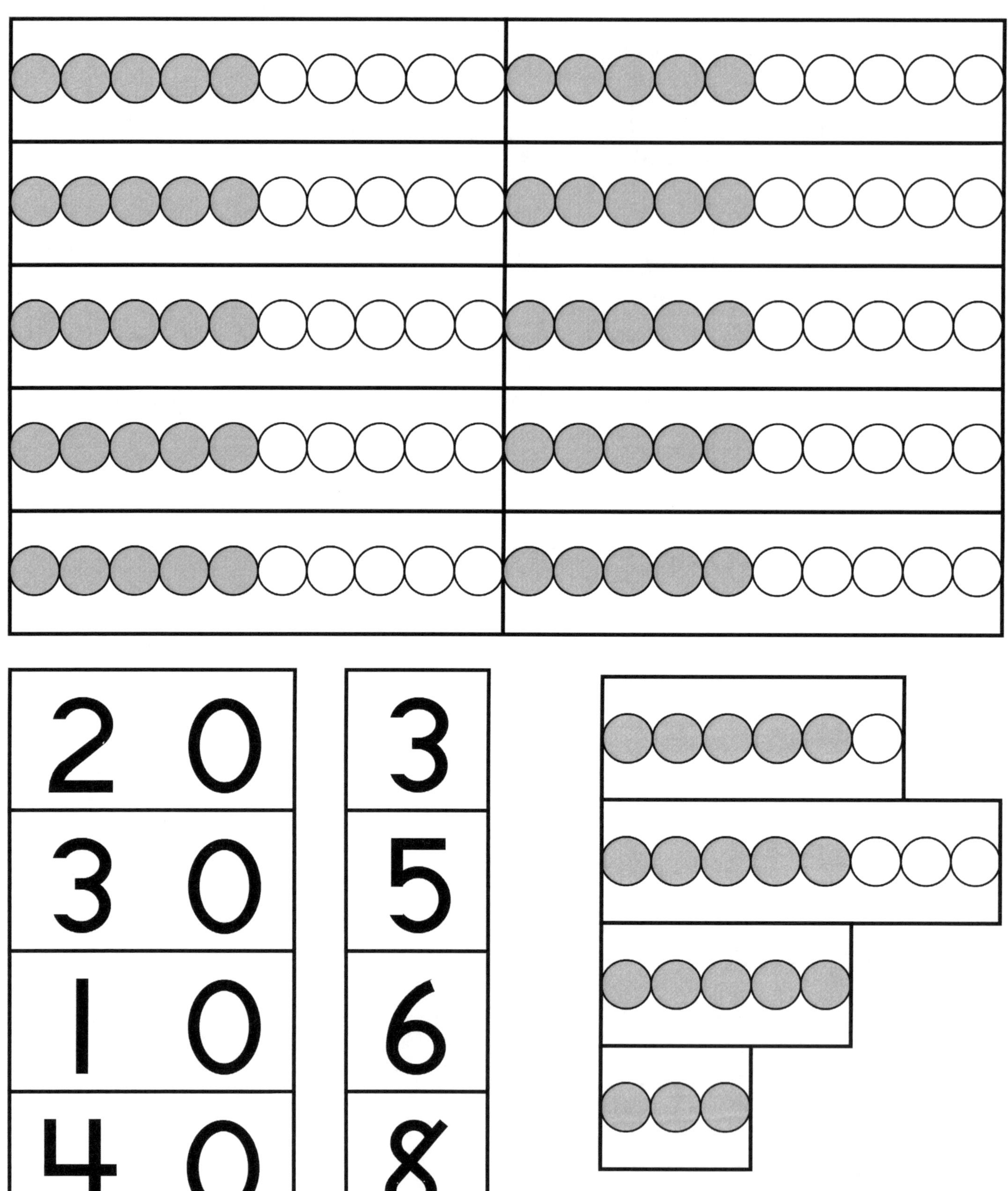

Worksheet 18, Adding Tens

Name

10 + 20 =

40 + 20 =

20 + 20 =

50 + 50 =

70 + 10 =

50 + 20 =

40 + 10 =

70 + 20 =

Worksheet 15, Adding Tens and Ones

Name

20 + 5 =

60 + 2 =

30 + 4 =

90 + 7 =

50 + 3 =

70 + 8 =

80 + 6 =

40 + 9 =

Name

Worksheet 19, Adding One to 2-Digit Numbers

Name ____________

43 + 1 =

17 + 1 =

88 + 1 =

35 + 1 =

66 + 1 =

29 + 1 =

54 + 1 =

79 + 1 =

Worksheet 20, Adding Two to 2-Digit Numbers

Name ____________

64 + 2 =

32 + 2 =

26 + 2 =

88 + 2 =

42 + 2 =

74 + 2 =

56 + 2 =

18 + 2 =

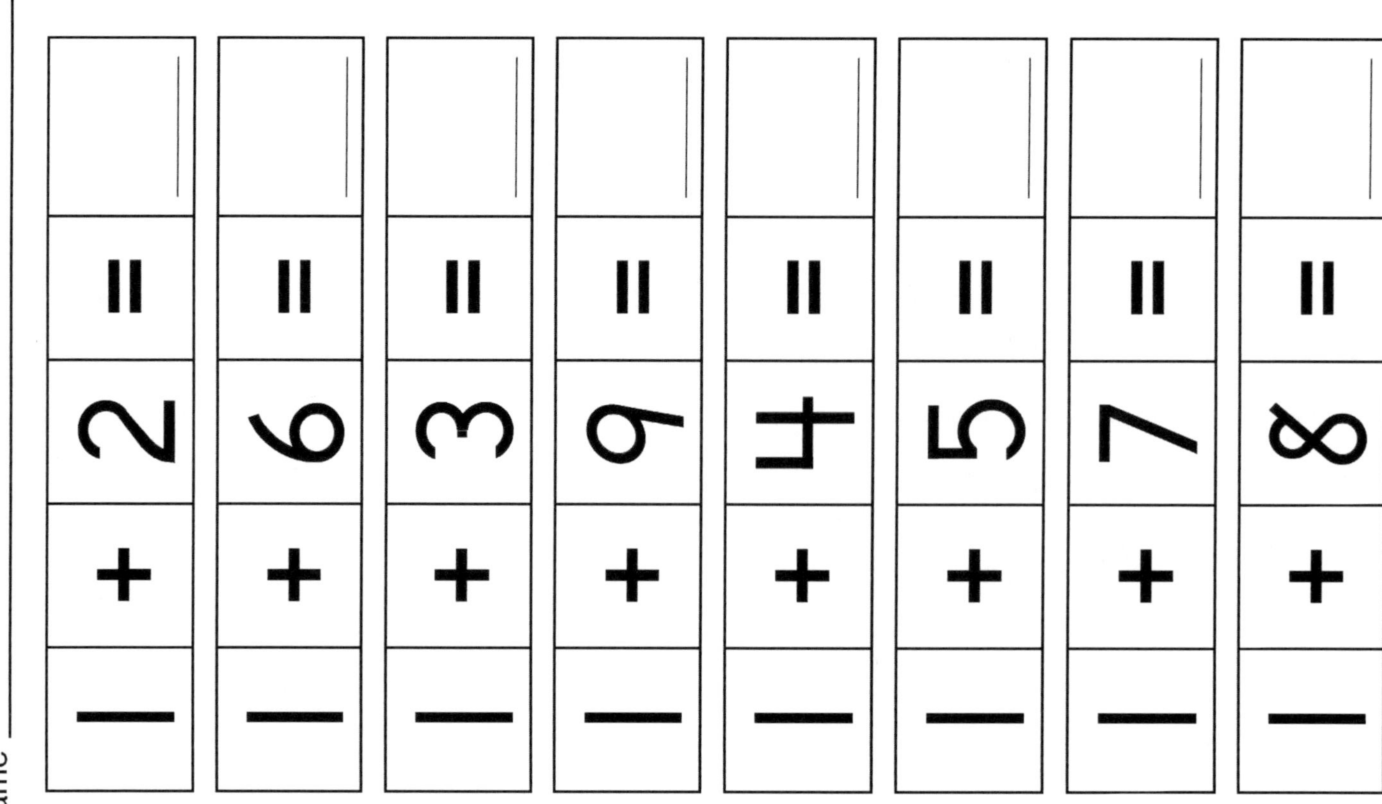

Name

Worksheet 21, The Commutative Property

Name

Name _______________

1 + 16 =

1 + 87 =

1 + 35 =

1 + 52 =

1 + 77 =

1 + 21 =

1 + 8 =

1 + 3 =

Worksheet 23, Counting by Twos

Name _______________

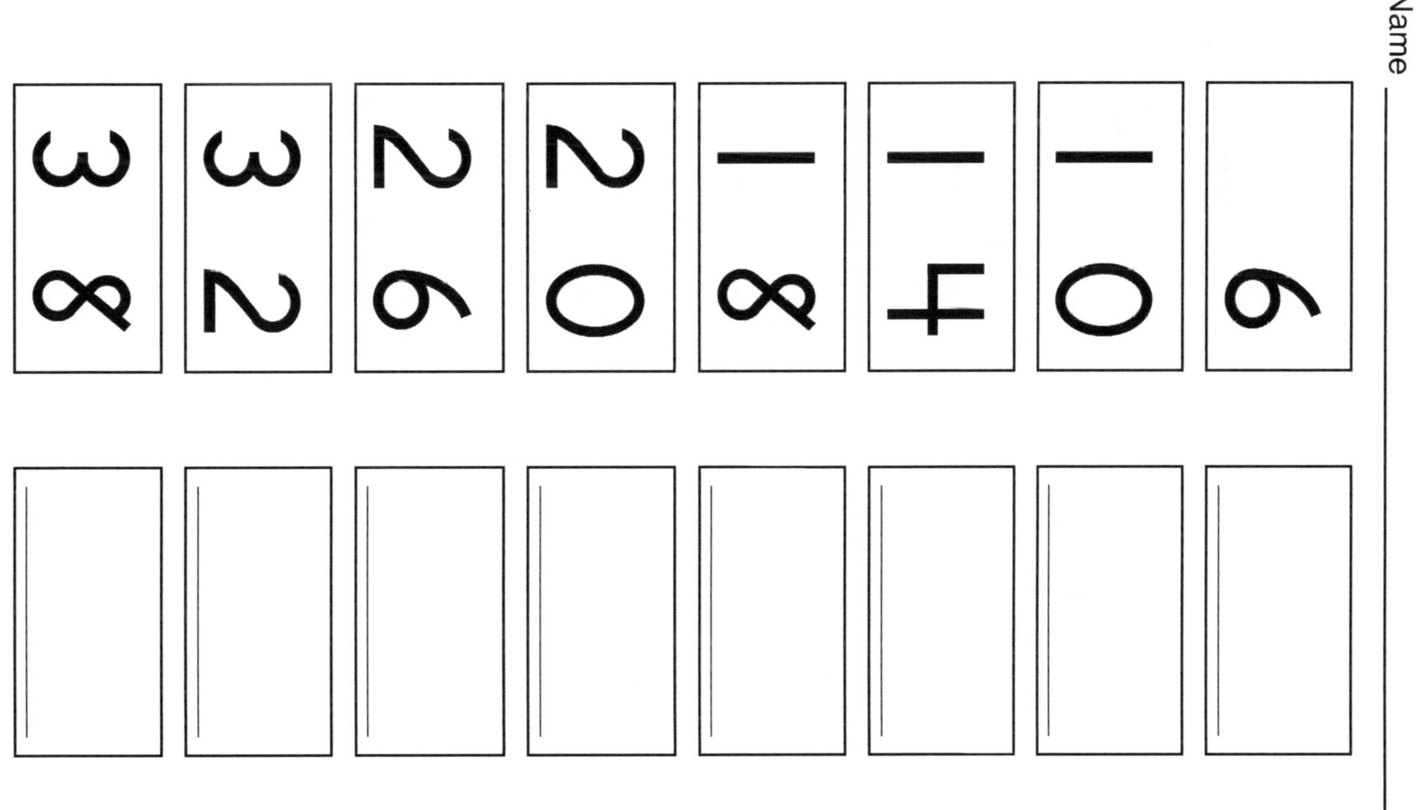

38

32

26

20

18

14

10

6

Name _______________________________________

1 0 0	=	7 0	+	
1 0 0	=	4 0	+	
1 0 0	=	5 0	+	
1 0 0	=	2 0	+	
1 0 0	=	9 0	+	
1 0 0	=	3 0	+	
1 0 0	=	8 0	+	
1 0 0	=	1 0	+	
1 0 0	=	6 0	+	
1 0 0	=	0	+	

Name _______________________________

1 5	=	1 0	+	
1 9	=	1 0	+	
1 3	=	1 0	+	
1 1	=	1 0	+	
1 7	=	1 0	+	
1 6	=	1 0	+	
1 4	=	1 0	+	
1 8	=	1 0	+	
1 2	=	1 0	+	
2 0	=	1 0	+	

Name _______________________________

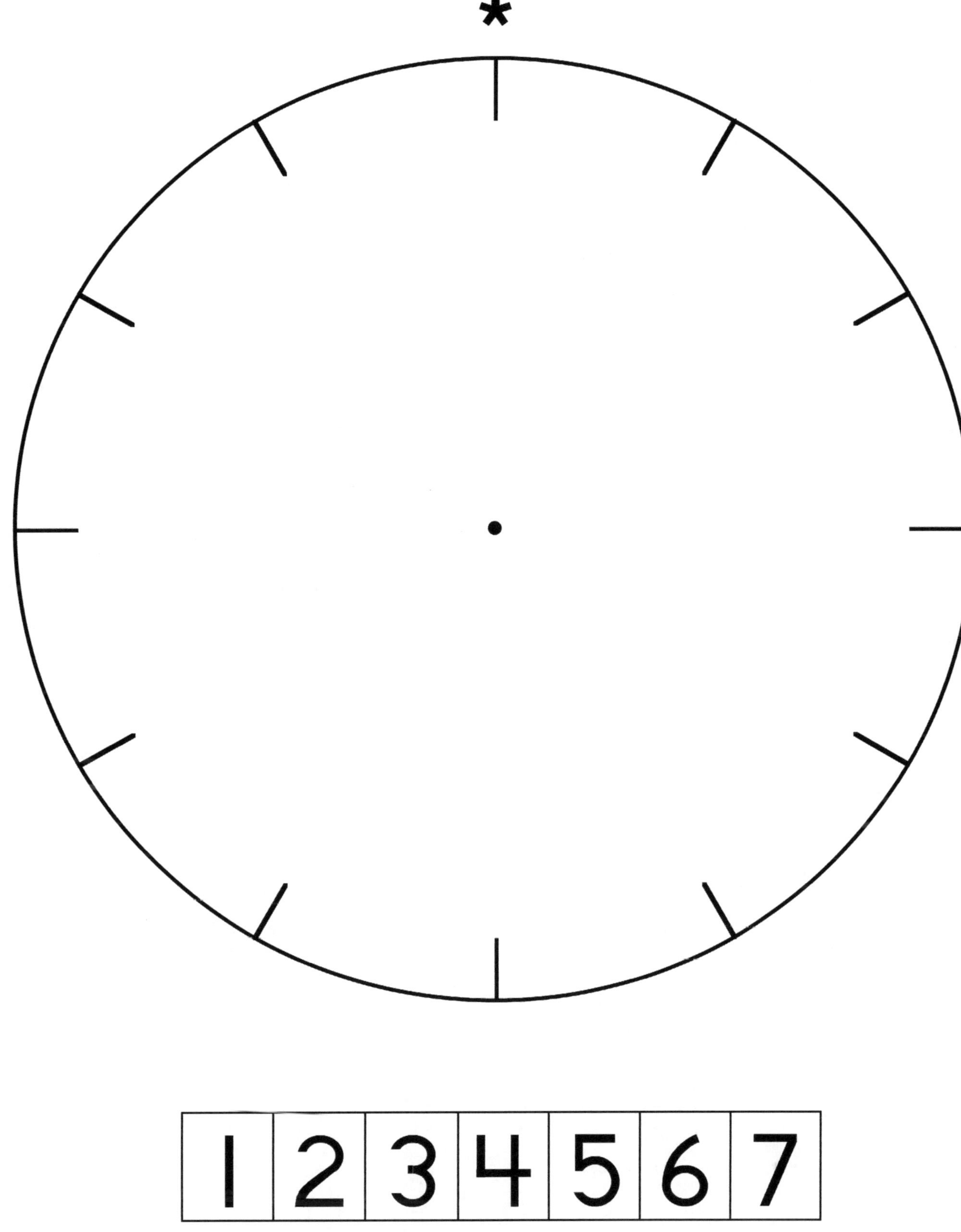

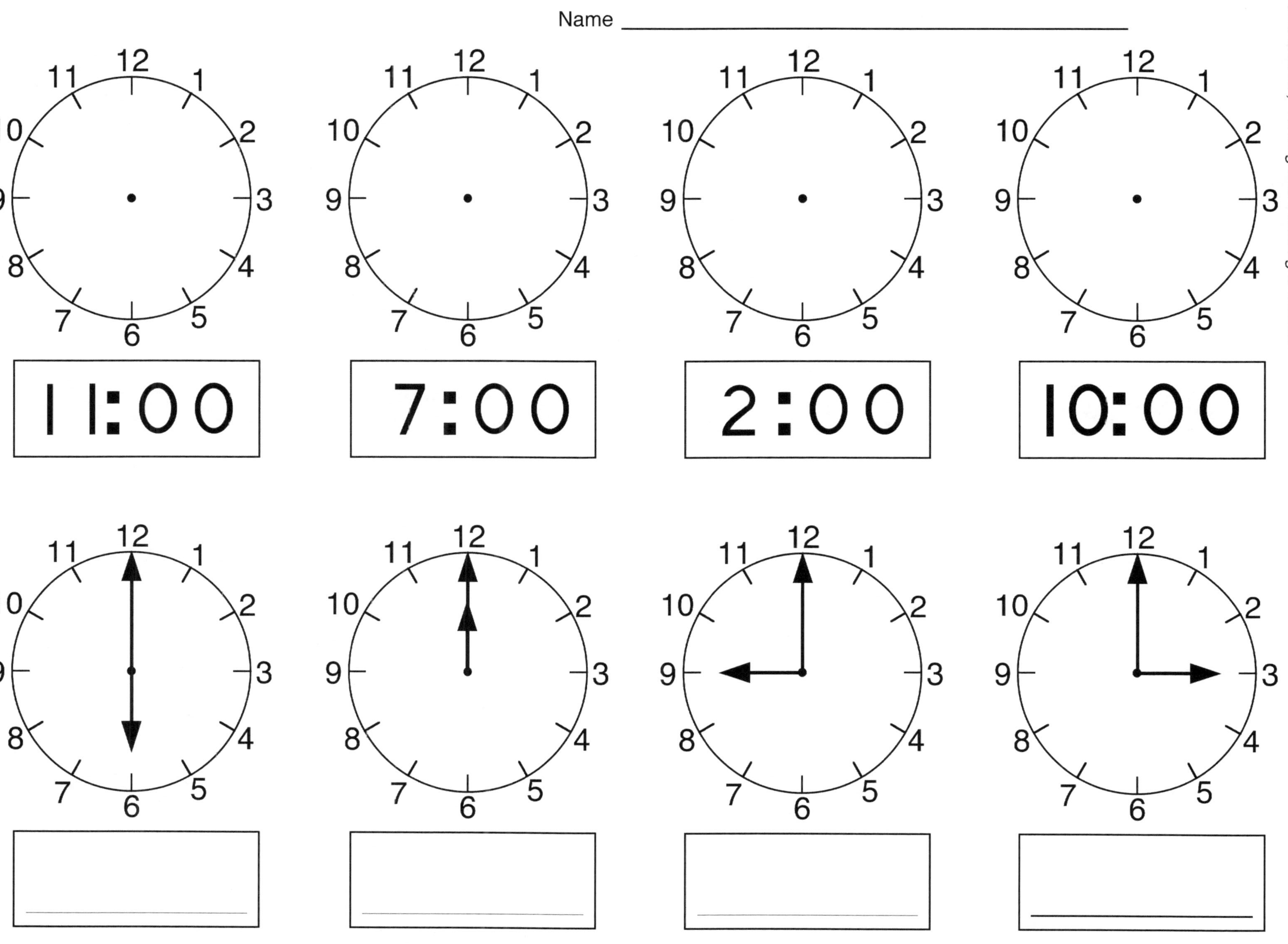

Name
Worksheet 27, Writing and Reading O'Clocks
11:00
7:00
2:00
10:00
K: © Joan A. Cotter 2001

Name _______________________

Find the crayons that are the same length and color them the same color.

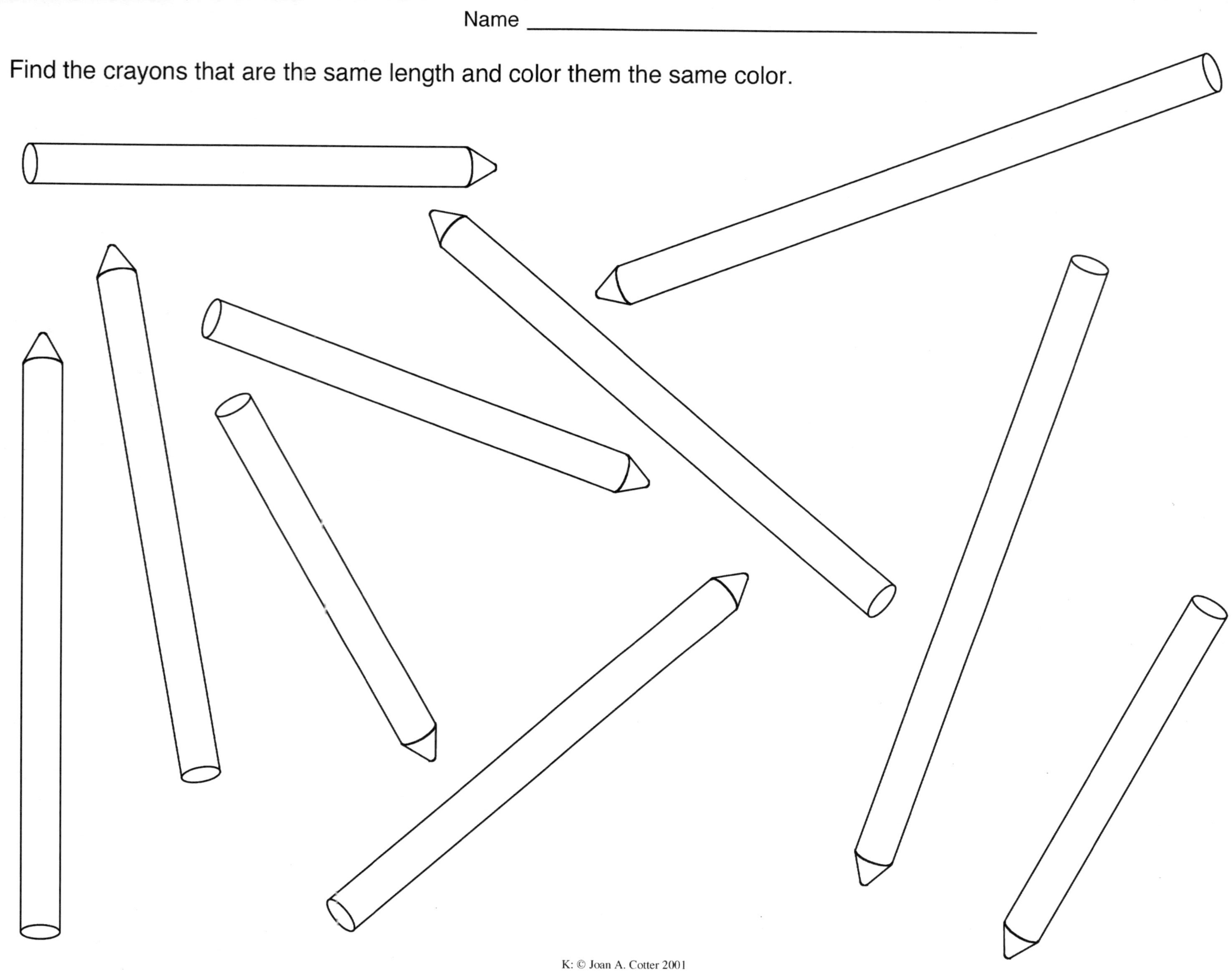